FREEDOM FIVE FORMULA

THE SIMPLE PATH TO FINANCIAL FREEDOM THROUGH REAL ESTATE

SDIRAWEALTH.COM

*To those who challenge the status quo—
who believe there's a better way,
who choose courage over comfort,
and who dare to dream of financial freedom
not someday, but starting today.*

This is for you.

Contents

The Path to Financial Freedom Starts Here

"The journey to financial freedom starts with a single decision: to take control of your future. Real estate is your vehicle, and the Freedom 5 Formula is your roadmap."

Imagine waking up every morning with the confidence that your financial future is secure. Picture yourself free from the worry of whether your savings will last through retirement, free from the stress of market downturns or unexpected expenses, and living a life where your money works for you.

For most people, that's just a dream. <u>But for you, this book holds the key to making it a reality.</u>

We're at a pivotal moment in history. The old ways of building wealth —relying on 401(k)s, pensions, and the stock market—are no longer working for the vast majority of people.

Millions of hard-working Americans retire with far less than they need, many finding themselves scraping by on a fraction of what they expected. But it doesn't have to be this way.

That's where the Freedom 5 Formula comes in. This isn't just another investment strategy—it's a step-by-step blueprint for achieving true financial independence.

It's designed for anyone, from complete beginners to experienced investors, and it simplifies real estate in a way that makes building lasting wealth not only achievable but inevitable.

In this book, you'll discover how acquiring just five properties—yes, just five—can set you up for life. With the right strategy, the right mindset, and the right approach, you can create a real estate portfolio that generates hundreds of thousands of dollars in passive income and builds over a million dollars in equity—all without sacrificing your current lifestyle.

But this book isn't just about money. It's about freedom.

The freedom to live life on your terms. The freedom to spend more time with your family, pursue your passions, and do the things that truly matter to you.

So let's begin this journey together. Keep reading, because the chapters ahead will equip you with the knowledge and the tools to not only transform your financial future but to live the life you've always dreamed of.

Chapter 1

The Retirement Reality Check: Why the Old Path is Failing You

"Goals without purpose are just wishes. When you know your 'why,' no obstacle is too great, and no dream is too big."

Let's face it: the traditional path to retirement is broken. For decades, we've been told that if we save diligently, contribute to our 401(k)s, and invest in the stock market, we'll be able to retire comfortably. But more and more people are realizing that this simply isn't true.

Here's the cold, hard truth: most Americans will never retire the way they hope to. Despite working 40 to 50 hours a week for decades, the average retiree has less than $250,000 saved—barely enough to cover basic living expenses for more than a few years. With experts suggesting that $1 million is the bare minimum for a comfortable retirement, it's no wonder so many people are worried about their financial future.

What's worse, traditional investments like stocks, bonds, and mutual funds aren't delivering the returns people expect. The stock market is unpredictable, and many people are seeing returns that barely outpace inflation. Then there's the risk—market crashes, political instability, and economic crises can wipe out years of savings in the blink of an eye.

But what if there was a way to break free from this uncertainty? What if you didn't have to rely on a system that's failing so many?

The Freedom 5 Formula is your way out. It's a strategy that doesn't just help you retire—it helps you thrive. With this formula, you can build a financial future where your money grows, your income is stable, and your wealth is protected from the unpredictability of traditional investments.

Why Real Estate is the Key to Financial Freedom

For over 4,000 years, real estate has been a cornerstone of wealth creation. It's no coincidence that the richest people in history—from the landlords of ancient Rome to the billionaires of today—built their fortunes through property ownership. Why? Because real estate offers something that few other investments can: stability, growth, and cash flow.

Unlike stocks, which rise and fall with the whims of the market, real estate is tangible. It's an asset you can see, touch, and improve. But more importantly, it's an asset that pays you back month after month. When you own property, you aren't just waiting for it to appreciate in value. You're earning rental income, building equity, and benefiting from the tax advantages that only real estate can offer.

And here's the best part: with the Freedom 5 Formula, you don't need to own 50 properties or be a millionaire to make real estate work for you. 90% of people only need five properties—just five—to build a life of financial security and abundance.

What's Waiting for You on the Other Side

Imagine this: you own five properties, generating enough rental income to cover your living expenses. Your tenants are effectively paying down your mortgages, increasing your equity month after month. Every year, your properties appreciate in value, while your cash flow grows stronger. Eventually the properties are paid off by the tenants and you now have cashflow you can live on. You're no longer dependent on a paycheck, no longer worrying about your 401(k) balance or the latest stock market crash.

Instead, you're free. Free to pursue the things you love. Free to travel. Free to spend more time with your family. Free to retire early, or not at all, because your financial future is secure.

This isn't just a pipe dream. It's the reality for those who follow the Freedom 5 Formula. And it can be your reality, too.

But achieving this kind of financial freedom requires more than just a desire for change—it requires action. It requires commitment. It requires you to take control of your financial destiny, rather than leaving it in the hands of a broken system.

This book will show you exactly how to do that. Step by step, I'll walk you through the process of acquiring your first property, building your portfolio, and ultimately achieving the kind of financial independence that most people only dream of.

Are you ready to take the first step?

What's Ahead in This Book

In the chapters ahead, we'll cover:

• How to Break Free from the Traditional Retirement Trap: Why relying on savings and the stock market is setting you up for failure—and what you can do instead.

• The Freedom 5 Formula Explained: We'll dive deep into the strategy that can turn five properties into $1.8 million in equity and $100,000 in annual passive income.

• Financing Strategies for Every Investor: Whether you're starting with no money or already have some capital, we'll explore creative ways to fund your real estate journey.

• Building Your Real Estate Dream Team: You can't do this alone, and you don't have to. Learn how to assemble a team of experts who will help you succeed at every step.

• Mastering the Art of Property Management: From finding tenants to maintaining your properties, we'll cover how to ensure your investments stay profitable and hassle-free.

• Maximizing Cash Flow and Accelerating Your Success: We'll show you how to use the rental income from your properties to aggressively pay down your loans, so you can own them free and clear as quickly as possible.

• Achieving True Financial Freedom: By the end of this book, you'll have a clear plan for not only achieving financial independence but creating a legacy of wealth for future generations.

This is your moment. You have the opportunity right now to step away from the uncertainty of traditional investments and step toward a future of financial freedom. The journey may not be easy, but it will be worth it. Let the Freedom 5 Formula be your guide.

Your financial freedom is within reach—are you ready to claim it?

Chapter 2

The Power of Real Estate

"Every empire begins with the first cornerstone. Your first property isn't just an investment—it's the foundation of your financial future."

When it comes to building long-term wealth, few investment vehicles have stood the test of time like real estate. For thousands of years, owning property has been synonymous with security, prosperity, and power. From the wealthy landowners of ancient civilizations to modern real estate moguls, property ownership has remained one of the most reliable ways to generate income and create lasting wealth.

But what is it that makes real estate so powerful, and why does it consistently outperform other forms of investment?

Why Real Estate?

Stocks rise and fall. Bonds offer minimal returns. Even gold, once seen as the ultimate hedge, fluctuates with global market forces. But real estate remains constant. Why? Because while other investments depend on abstract values, real estate is tangible. It's something you can touch, improve, and control. And unlike the stock market, where your success depends on factors completely outside your control, real estate offers a level of stability and predictability that's hard to match.

"Real estate investing is for those who want more influence and control over their retirement."

Here's why real estate is your ticket to financial freedom:

1. Cash Flow

From day one, real estate provides something no other investment does: monthly income. When you own rental properties, you generate consistent, reliable cash flow. Every month, your tenants pay you rent, and that rent covers your expenses—your mortgage, property management fees, taxes, and insurance—and leaves you with positive cash flow in your pocket.

Over time, this cash flow only grows. As rents increase and mortgages get paid down, the gap between what you collect and what you pay out widens, giving you more passive income each year. And the best part? Once your mortgage is paid off, that cash flow becomes pure profit.

2. Appreciation

Real estate values tend to rise over time. While the market experiences ups and downs, property values have consistently increased over the long term. Every year, your investment appreciates, adding more to your net worth without you lifting a finger. If you're holding properties in high-growth markets, appreciation can significantly outpace the returns of other investments.

3. Principal Paydown

As your tenants pay rent, they're also helping you pay off your mortgage. Each month, a portion of that payment goes toward reducing your loan balance. This is called principal paydown, and it's one of the most overlooked yet powerful aspects of real estate investing. Over time, as the loan balance decreases, your equity in the property increases. This means you're building wealth even while you sleep, simply by owning the property.

4. Tax Benefits

One of the greatest advantages of real estate investing is the tax benefits. From depreciation to mortgage interest deductions, real estate allows you to lower your taxable income while your properties appreciate and generate cash flow.

These deductions effectively put more money in your pocket each year, accelerating your path to financial freedom. We'll dive into these tax benefits in more detail later, but for now, just know that real estate offers unmatched advantages when it comes to reducing your tax liability.

5. Leverage

Perhaps the greatest strength of real estate is leverage. With real estate, you can control a much larger asset with relatively little upfront capital. Imagine this: you purchase a $230,000 property with a 25% down payment, meaning you only put up $57,500.

However, you're not just earning returns on your $57,500—you're earning on the entire value of the property, $230,000. The ability to use the bank's money to build your portfolio allows you to grow your wealth far more quickly than if you were investing your own money in full.

6. Protection Against Inflation

In times of inflation, the purchasing power of your cash decreases. But with real estate, rents and property values tend to rise with inflation.

This means your investment not only maintains its value but also increases over time, making real estate a powerful hedge against inflation. In contrast, money sitting in a savings account loses value every year, and other investments may not keep pace with rising costs.

What Sets Real Estate Apart?

Control. When you invest in real estate, you are in control of your investment.

You can choose where and what type of property to buy, what improvements to make, and how to manage it.

In contrast, when you invest in stocks or bonds, your money is in the hands of corporate executives or government decisions.

Real estate allows you to make strategic moves that can increase your returns. You can raise rents, renovate properties to increase value, and decide when to sell or refinance to tap into your equity.

Multiple Streams of Income. Real estate doesn't rely on a single stream of income. It generates wealth through cash flow, appreciation, principal paydown, tax benefits, and leverage—all working together to accelerate your wealth-building process.

With stocks or mutual funds, your only income source is capital appreciation, which you can't access without selling your investment. Real estate, on the other hand, lets you benefit from multiple streams, increasing both your cash flow and your overall net worth simultaneously.

Why New Construction?

In the Freedom 5 Formula, we focus on new construction properties, but why?

1. Lower Maintenance Costs

New construction properties come with fewer maintenance issues than older properties. Everything is brand new, from the roof to the plumbing, so you won't be dealing with expensive repairs. This translates to fewer surprises and more predictable cash flow.

2. Attract Better Tenants

Tenants are drawn to new construction properties. New homes offer modern layouts, updated amenities, and energy-efficient appliances, making them highly desirable. This means you'll likely attract higher-quality tenants who are willing to pay a premium for living in a newly built home.

3. Higher Rents

Because new construction properties are in higher demand, you can charge higher rents. This leads to better cash flow and helps you pay down your mortgage faster, getting you to financial freedom sooner.

4. Built in High-Growth Areas

Developers typically build new construction homes in areas experiencing growth—places where job opportunities are increasing, populations are rising, and local economies are thriving. These are the markets that tend to appreciate faster, giving you both immediate cash flow and long-term appreciation.

Why Only Five Properties?

You might be wondering: Why five properties? Why not ten or twenty?

The answer is simple: Most people only need five properties to achieve financial freedom.

While it's possible to scale up and own more, the Freedom 5 Formula is designed to help you retire comfortably with a manageable, sustainable portfolio.

With just five properties, you can generate enough cash flow to cover your living expenses, build over a million dollars in equity, and create a stable income stream that lasts through retirement.

Five properties may not sound like much, but it's enough to transform your financial future. It's achievable, manageable, and powerful.

And the best part?

Once you've reached five, you can choose to keep going and scale your portfolio, or simply enjoy the freedom you've created.

The Path Forward

By now, you're beginning to understand why real estate is a formidable tool for wealth building. The true magic unfolds when you merge real estate's benefits with the Freedom 5 Formula. In the upcoming chapter, we'll dive into how this formula operates, step by step.

You'll discover how to acquire your first property, how to leverage rental cash flow to expedite debt repayment, and how to reach financial independence quicker than you imagined.

Successful investors emphasize building wealth over seeking immediate cash flow because they recognize that wealth offers long-term financial security and growth opportunities. Wealth building involves accumulating assets that rise in value over time. These assets not only appreciate, yielding significant profits when sold or liquidated, but they often also produce cash flow!

When investors concentrate on wealth building, they tend to make strategic, informed decisions about resource allocation. They craft a portfolio that matches their long-term financial goals and risk tolerance, often diversifying to reduce potential losses. This approach contrasts with focusing solely on cash flow, which might lead to high-risk investments for quick returns, potentially jeopardizing long-term wealth accumulation.

By prioritizing wealth creation, successful investors grasp that cash flow is a natural consequence. For example, owning a portfolio of real estate properties not only enhances wealth through property appreciation but also generates rental income, providing consistent cash flow. Similarly, investing in dividend-paying stocks contributes to cash flow while the underlying asset appreciates.

Ultimately, the mindset of building wealth first is about maintaining a long-term view, utilizing the power of compound interest, and taking calculated risks, all while ensuring steady cash flow that supports ongoing investments and provides financial stability.

Chapter 3

The Foundation of the Freedom 5 Formula: Your Path to Financial Independence

"True wealth isn't built overnight; it's forged through patience, consistency, and time. Each day your investments grow, your future becomes more secure, and your financial freedom closer than ever."

Step-by-Step: How the Freedom 5 Formula Works

Now that you've grasped the core concepts behind the Freedom 5 Formula, it's time to break it down into actionable steps.

This formula is designed to be simple yet powerful, guiding you through building a real estate portfolio that will secure your financial freedom.

The journey begins by focusing on three foundational pillars: Purpose-Driven Goals, Building the Right Team, and Acquiring Five New Construction Properties. Here's how it all comes together.

Step 1: Set Purpose-Driven Goals

Before diving into real estate investing, it's critical to have a clear vision of what you want to accomplish and your "why."

Ask yourself:

What does financial freedom mean to you? Is it retiring early, traveling the world, or ensuring your family's future security?

Having well-defined goals gives you clarity and focus.

It's your "why" that will motivate you when challenges arise and keep you on track to success.

Your goals should be specific and measurable. For example, you might aim to generate $100,000 in passive income annually, own five mortgage-free properties within 15 years, or build a legacy of wealth to pass down to future generations.

Knowing exactly what you want to achieve helps guide your decisions and keeps you committed to the process.

Step 2: Build the Right Team

The next key step is assembling a strong team of experts to help you achieve your goals. Real estate is a team sport, and having the right people by your side can make or break your success.

You need a team that understands new construction properties and has experience in targeting high-growth markets.

Here's the kind of team you need to build:

- Real Estate Advisors: Specialists who know the markets, understand property values, and can guide you toward high-performing new construction properties designed to generate positive cash flow from day one.

- Financial Advisors: Experts who can help you with securing financing, using strategies like leveraging your existing assets, HELOCs, or even self-directed IRAs. They'll ensure you have the right financial structure to maximize returns.

- Property Management Team: A professional property manager will take care of finding tenants, handling maintenance, and making sure your investment is running smoothly without day-to-day involvement from you.

By working with an experienced team, you avoid the pitfalls that many first-time investors face and ensure that your investments are strategic, profitable, and easy to manage.

Step 3: Acquire Five New Construction Properties

The heart of the Freedom 5 Formula is acquiring five new construction properties in high-growth markets. These properties offer significant advantages over older, rehabbed homes, such as lower maintenance costs, better-quality tenants, and more predictable cash flow.

When you focus on new builds, you minimize your headaches and maximize your profits.

Here's how to start:

• Choose the Right Markets: Focus on high-growth cities or regions with strong job markets, rising populations, and healthy rental demand. This ensures both appreciation in property value and consistent rental income.

• Secure Financing: Use smart financing strategies to acquire your properties. Leverage mortgages, HELOCs, or self-directed IRAs to control a large asset with minimal upfront capital, allowing you to grow your portfolio faster.

• Purchase Properties that Generate Cash Flow: Each property you acquire should immediately start generating positive cash flow. This ensures your investments are self-sustaining from day one, allowing you to use the cash flow to reinvest into growing your portfolio.

Step 4: Maximize Cash Flow and Use It to Pay Down Loans

Once your five properties are in place, the real power of the Freedom 5 Formula kicks in. The goal here is to maximize your cash flow and aggressively pay down your loans. Every dollar of cash flow generated from your properties should go toward accelerating your mortgage payments.

The faster you pay off your loans, the faster you'll own these properties free and clear.

Here's how it works:

- Positive Cash Flow: Ensure that after all expenses—mortgages, taxes, insurance, and property management—you're still generating positive cash flow each month. For example, if each property generates $500 a month in net cash flow, that's $2,500 per month across five properties.

- Reinvest Cash Flow into Loan Payoff: Rather than using your cash flow for personal expenses, reinvest it to pay down the principal on your mortgages. This will help you pay off your properties faster, potentially cutting your mortgage terms in half.

Once your properties are paid off, your cash flow will explode. Without mortgage payments, you'll go from earning $500 per property per month to earning $1,500 or more. That's $7,500 in monthly passive income from five properties—setting you up for financial freedom.

Step 5: Enjoy the Benefits of Long-Term Wealth

With your properties now mortgage-free and producing significant cash flow, you've built a self-sustaining portfolio that generates passive income each month. But it doesn't end there. As time goes on, your properties will appreciate in value, and your rental income will rise with inflation, further increasing your wealth.

What's even better? You've not only secured your financial future but have created a legacy of wealth that you can pass on to your family. The Freedom 5 Formula is not just about today—it's about building wealth that lasts generations.

The Roadmap to Financial Freedom

The Freedom 5 Formula is designed to be simple, effective, and transformational. By focusing on purpose-driven goals, leveraging the expertise of a strong team, and acquiring five carefully selected new construction properties, you're laying the groundwork for a lifetime of financial security. Each step of the formula builds on the last, taking you closer to your ultimate goal of financial independence.

Now, let's dive deeper into how you can fund your real estate purchases, how to build the perfect real estate team, and how to optimize your returns through smart investing strategies. You've already taken the first step by committing to this journey—now let's keep the momentum going and work toward creating the life of financial freedom you've always dreamed of.

The journey starts now.

Chapter 4

The Three Phases of the Freedom 5 Formula

"Financial freedom is achieved in phases—each step builds upon the last, leading you closer to a life where your wealth works for you. Trust the process, follow the formula, and watch your future unfold."

At this point, you know that the Freedom 5 Formula is your path to financial independence, but how do you get there?

In this chapter, we'll break the process down into three simple phases: Acquire, Leverage, and Cash Flow. These phases guide you through the journey of building wealth with real estate, helping you focus on the right steps at the right time.

Each phase has its own milestones, challenges, and rewards. Whether you're just starting out with your first property or you're already on your way to owning five, understanding these phases will help you stay on track and achieve the financial freedom you're aiming for.

Phase 1: Acquire Your Properties and Build Your Portfolio

Timeframe: 1-5 Years to acquire your portfolio

The first phase of the Freedom 5 Formula is all about acquisition. This is where the groundwork is laid, and your journey truly begins. Over the course of 1-5 years, your goal is to acquire five new construction properties that will form the foundation of your real estate portfolio. The goal would be 1 property a year.

Here's why we focus on acquisition early on: the faster you acquire your properties, the quicker you can start generating cash flow and paying down debt. The sooner you begin, the sooner you'll be able to enjoy the benefits of long-term wealth. During this phase, your attention will be on finding the right properties, securing financing, and building your team of real estate professionals.

What to Focus On in Phase 1:

• Identifying High-Growth Markets: Start by researching and identifying markets where property values are rising, job growth is strong, and rental demand is high. These are the areas that will offer the best chances for appreciation and consistent rental income. Your real estate agent and property management team can help you find opportunities that fit your criteria.

• Financing Smartly: You don't need to pay for properties outright—that's where the power of leverage comes in. By using the bank's money (through mortgages), you can control properties worth much more than your initial investment. We'll dive deeper into financing strategies in the next chapter, but for now, focus on securing financing that allows you to maximize your cash flow from day one.

• Scaling Quickly: Once you've purchased your first property, don't stop. Use the cash flow and equity from that property to fund your next purchase. The faster you acquire your five properties, the faster you can move on to the next phase of the formula.

Mindset for Phase 1:

Think of Phase 1 as the building phase. It's the most hands-on part of your journey, and it requires discipline, focus, and determination. But once you've acquired your five properties, you've crossed a major milestone on your path to financial independence. From here, it only gets easier. You've built the foundation—now it's time to watch your wealth grow.

Phase 2: Leverage Time in the Market

Timeframe: 10-15 Years to leverage time in the market pay off your portfolio

Once you've acquired your five properties, you enter the second phase of the Freedom 5 Formula: leveraging time in the market. This phase is where the magic of real estate really starts to work for you. It's about patience, discipline, and allowing time to do the heavy lifting as your properties appreciate and your mortgages get paid down.

The beauty of real estate investing is that, over time, your wealth compounds. As your tenants pay rent, they're paying down your mortgage. As property values increase, your equity grows. All of this happens without you needing to constantly monitor the market or make frequent trades—unlike the stock market. In this phase, you focus on maintaining your properties, optimizing cash flow, and keeping your eye on the long-term goal.

What to Focus On in Phase 2:

- Aggressively Pay Down Your Debt: Use the cash flow from your five properties to pay down your mortgage loans faster. This is one of the key components of the Freedom 5 Formula. By making extra payments toward your mortgage principal, you can cut years off the life of your loan. Every dollar you use to pay down debt accelerates your journey to owning mortgage-free properties.

- Let the Market Work for You: Real estate isn't about timing the market—it's about time in the market. The longer you hold your properties, the more they appreciate, and the more equity you build. During this phase, you're positioning yourself for massive financial gains by holding onto your properties as they increase in value.

- Minimize Vacancies: Work closely with your property manager to ensure that your properties stay rented. High-quality tenants mean steady rental income, and steady rental income means you're consistently paying down your mortgage and generating cash flow.

Mindset for Phase 2:

This phase requires patience. You're not flipping properties or chasing quick wins. You're letting your portfolio grow in value over time, while focusing on increasing cash flow and paying down debt. The real estate market rewards those who hold on to properties for the long haul, and you'll be amazed at how quickly your wealth can multiply if you stay the course.

Phase 3: Enjoy Cash Flow and Financial Freedom

Timeframe: Endless

The final phase of the Freedom 5 Formula is where everything comes together. By this point, you've paid off your mortgages, and you now own five properties free and clear. This means your cash flow skyrockets—without a mortgage to pay each month, the majority of your rental income becomes pure profit.

At this stage, you have reached true financial freedom. Your properties are generating enough income to cover your living expenses and provide a comfortable lifestyle. You have the option to retire, continue growing your portfolio, or use your wealth to pursue other passions. The best part? You're no longer relying on a paycheck, and your financial future is secure. You took control and created this for you and your family.

What to Focus On in Phase 3:

- Maximize Your Cash Flow: With no mortgage payments, your cash flow will be at its peak. Continue managing your properties well and optimizing rent rates to ensure you're getting the most out of each property.

- Consider Expanding Your Portfolio: While five properties are enough to provide financial freedom, many investors choose to continue growing their portfolios. You can use the cash flow from your existing properties to purchase additional real estate, further increasing your income and wealth.

- Enjoy Your Freedom: You've worked hard, and now it's time to enjoy the rewards. Whether that means traveling the world, spending more time with your family, or starting a new venture, this phase is about living life on your terms.

Mindset for Phase 3:

You've made it! By following the Freedom 5 Formula, you've built a portfolio of mortgage-free properties that provide significant cash flow and wealth. At this point, your focus shifts from building wealth to enjoying it. You're in control of your financial future, and you have the freedom to live the life you've always dreamed of.

The Power of Staying the Course

The Freedom 5 Formula is a long-term strategy, but its rewards are worth every bit of effort and patience. It's easy to get distracted by short-term gains, but by focusing on the three phases—Acquire, Leverage, and Cash Flow—you're setting yourself up for success that lasts a lifetime.

There will be challenges along the way, but with the right mindset and the right team in place, you can achieve financial independence faster than you ever thought possible. The key is to stay the course, remain disciplined, and trust the process. Real estate has been a proven wealth-building tool for centuries, and the Freedom 5 Formula makes it accessible, achievable, and life-changing.

In the next chapters, we'll dive deeper into the strategies and tools you can use to acquire your properties, finance your portfolio, and manage your real estate empire. By the time you've finished this book, you'll have everything you need to start your journey toward financial freedom.

Chapter 5

The Math Behind the Magic—How the Freedom 5 Formula Multiplies Your Wealth

"The magic of momentum turns small steps into giant leaps. Each property brings you closer to a life of abundance and independence."

Now that we've covered the overarching strategy, let's get into the numbers. If you're someone who likes to see exactly how wealth is built, this is the chapter for you.

The Freedom 5 Formula isn't just a good idea—it's grounded in real numbers that consistently show why real estate is one of the most powerful wealth-building tools in existence.

The math behind this formula is simple but incredibly powerful.

With just five properties, you can create a financial empire that generates enough passive income to support your lifestyle and builds over a million dollars in equity.

Ready to see how it all adds up? Let's dive in.

The Starting Point: Acquiring Your Properties

We're going to start by assuming you've acquired five properties, each valued at $230,000. Don't worry if this number feels high or low for your local market—what's important is understanding how the formula works, and we can always adjust these numbers to fit your unique situation.

To purchase each of these properties, we'll assume you're putting down 25%, which is typical for investment properties.

That means you're investing $57,500 for each property, for a total upfront investment of $287,500 across all five.

Let's break this down:

- Property Value: $230,000 per property
- Down Payment (25%): $57,500 per property
- Total Investment: $287,500 across all five properties

At this stage, you now control $1,150,000 in real estate for an upfront investment of just $287,500.

This is the power of leverage.

You're using other people's money—mainly the bank's—to control a large asset base, and as we'll see, this leverage is what will allow your wealth to grow exponentially.

The Power of Cash Flow

Once you've acquired your five properties, the next step is generating cash flow. Cash flow is the money you collect from rent after covering all your expenses, including mortgage payments, property management fees, insurance, taxes, and maintenance costs.

Let's assume each property rents for $1,600 per month. This gives you a total rental income of $8,000 per month across your five properties.

But, of course, not all of this is profit. You have to cover your mortgage, taxes, and other expenses. Here's a basic breakdown of your monthly costs:

- Mortgage Payment (Principal + Interest): $900 per property

- Taxes + Insurance: $200 per property

- Property Management + Maintenance: $100 per property

So, your total monthly expenses for each property are approximately $1,200.

This leaves you with $400 in positive cash flow per property, or $2,000 in total monthly cash flow across all five properties.

Monthly Cash Flow Breakdown:

- Rental Income: $1,600 per property ($8,000 total)

- Total Expenses: $1,200 per property ($6,000 total)

- Net Monthly Cash Flow: $400 per property ($2,000 total)

That's an additional $2,000 of passive income coming in every single month. Over the course of a year, that's $24,000 in passive income.

But that's just the beginning.

The Power of Principal Paydown

One of the hidden benefits of real estate investing is principal paydown. Every month, part of your mortgage payment goes toward paying down the principal balance on your loan.

This means that while your tenants are paying rent, they're also effectively paying off your mortgage for you.

Let's assume that out of your $900 monthly mortgage payment, about $300 goes toward reducing the principal on the loan.

That's $300 per property, or $1,500 per month across all five properties.

Principal Paydown Breakdown:

- Principal Reduction: $300 per property

- Total Principal Paydown (5 properties):

    $1,500 per month ($18,000 per year)

So, in addition to your $2,000 in monthly cash flow, you're also gaining $1,500 in equity each month as your tenants pay down your loans.

Over the course of a year, that's $18,000 in equity growth just from principal paydown.

Appreciation: The Silent Wealth Builder

Real estate doesn't just provide cash flow and equity through principal paydown—it also appreciates in value over time.

While appreciation rates vary by market, the national average has historically been around 3-5% per year.

Let's be conservative and assume your properties appreciate at 3% per year.

With five properties valued at $230,000 each, that's an increase of $6,900 per property, or $34,500 in total appreciation each year.

Appreciation Breakdown:

- Property Value: $230,000

- Appreciation Rate: 3%

- Annual Appreciation per Property: $6,900

- Total Annual Appreciation (5 properties): $34,500

The Tax Benefits of Real Estate

One of the most overlooked benefits of real estate investing is the incredible tax advantages it provides.

The tax code is designed to encourage real estate investment, and savvy investors can take advantage of numerous deductions to reduce their taxable income and increase their cash flow.

Here are just a few of the key tax benefits you can enjoy as a real estate investor:

• Depreciation: The IRS allows you to depreciate the value of your rental property over time, even though the property is likely increasing in value. This non-cash expense can reduce your taxable income, allowing you to keep more of your rental income.

• Mortgage Interest Deduction: You can deduct the interest you pay on your mortgage, further reducing your taxable income.

• Operating Expense Deductions: Expenses such as property management fees, repairs, maintenance, and insurance are all tax-deductible, which can help offset your rental income and lower your tax liability.

Combined, these tax benefits can put thousands of dollars back in your pocket every year, increasing your overall returns and accelerating your path to financial freedom.

How It All Adds Up: The Power of Compounding Wealth

Let's bring all 4 streams of income together to showcase how cash flow, principal paydown, appreciation, depreciation, and tax benefits all work in concert to accelerate your wealth-building efforts. Real estate is unique in that it allows you to build wealth on multiple fronts simultaneously. Here's how the numbers break down over just one year:

Total Annual Wealth Building:

- Cash Flow: $24,000 per year ($2,000 per month)

    - Principal Paydown: $18,000 per year

    - Appreciation: $34,500 per year (assuming a 3% appreciation rate on a $1.15 million portfolio)

    - Standard Depreciation: $36,818 per year (based on $1,012,500 depreciated over 27.5 years)

    - Tax Savings from Depreciation:$36,818 x 0.37 (for 37% tax bracket) = $13,622 in tax savings per year

Total Annual Wealth-Building Calculation:

$24,000 (cash flow)

    - $18,000 (principal paydown)

    - $34,500 (appreciation)

    - $13,622 (tax savings from depreciation)

Total Wealth Building: $90,122 in the first year alone

In just one year, your real estate portfolio is generating over $90,000 in wealth. This is happening every year, and it compounds over time.

As rents increase, your cash flow grows. As property values rise, your equity multiplies. And as you continue to pay down your mortgages, your net worth soars.

The Long-Term Payoff: A Million-Dollar Portfolio

Let's fast-forward 10-15 years into the future, when you've paid off your mortgages and own your properties free and clear.

At this point, your rental income will have grown significantly, and your properties will likely have doubled in value.

Assuming a modest 3% annual appreciation rate, your five properties, originally worth $1,150,000, will now be worth around $1.8 million.

And with no mortgage payments, your cash flow will be close to $100,000 per year.

That's true financial freedom—a portfolio worth nearly $2 million and $100,000 in passive income every year, all from just five properties.

What This Means for You

The numbers don't lie. By following the Freedom 5 Formula, you can create a portfolio that builds wealth on multiple levels—through cash flow, principal paydown, appreciation, and tax benefits.

The formula is designed to help you reach financial freedom in a way that's simple, manageable, and incredibly powerful.

Now that you've seen the math behind the magic, the next step is to make it a reality. In the upcoming chapters, we'll dive deeper into financing strategies that will help you fund your investments and accelerate your portfolio's growth.

We'll also walk you through how to build your real estate dream team —from lenders to property managers—to ensure your journey to financial freedom is smooth and successful.

And just when you think it couldn't get any better, we'll unlock the secrets of advanced tax strategies specifically designed for high-net-worth investors.

Imagine slashing your tax bill in Year 1 with cost segregation, allowing you to keep more of your rental income, and using 1031 exchanges to defer capital gains taxes while continuously upgrading your portfolio.

These tools are what separate successful investors from the rest. In the upcoming tax chapter, we'll show you how to leverage these strategies to multiply your wealth faster than you thought possible.

Buckle up, because the road to financial independence is just beginning—and it's paved with powerful strategies that will put you in control of your financial future.

Chapter 6

Maximizing Wealth with Tax Strategies for High-Net-Worth Investors

"The smartest investors don't just make money—they keep it. Master the art of tax strategies, and unlock the full potential of your wealth."

For high-net-worth investors, advanced tax strategies are essential for maximizing wealth and reducing tax burdens. Real estate, particularly new construction properties, offers some of the most powerful tax advantages available.

In this chapter, we'll explore two key strategies that high-income earners, like doctors, lawyers, and business owners, can use to defer taxes and significantly increase their wealth over time. These strategies include cost segregation and 1031 exchanges, which allow investors to unlock substantial tax savings and accelerate portfolio growth.

Using the same numbers from Chapter 5, we'll demonstrate how these strategies can be applied to a five-property portfolio valued at $1.5 million and how they can generate significant tax savings in the first year and beyond.

Cost Segregation: Accelerating Depreciation for Maximum Tax Savings

Cost segregation is an advanced tax strategy that allows real estate investors to front-load their depreciation deductions by reclassifying certain parts of their property into shorter depreciation schedules. For high-net-worth investors, this strategy can be a game-changer—providing substantial tax savings in the early years of property ownership, freeing up cash flow, and reinvesting those savings for accelerated growth.

How Cost Segregation Works for High-Income Investors

Normally, residential real estate is depreciated over 27.5 years. This means that a portion of the property's value is deducted from your taxable income each year. However, with cost segregation, many building components—such as electrical systems, plumbing, and fixtures—can be depreciated over 5, 7, or 15 years, allowing you to accelerate these deductions and realize significant tax savings upfront.

For high-income earners in the 37% tax bracket, the ability to take larger deductions in the first year can dramatically reduce their tax liability. Let's take a closer look at how this would work in Year 1.

<u>Year 1 Tax Savings with Cost Segregation</u>

Assume you have purchased five new construction properties with the following details:
- Total Purchase Price (5 Properties): $1,500,000
- Building Value: $1,350,000 (90% of purchase price; land is 10%)
- Accelerated Depreciation (via Cost Segregation Study): 25% of building value

Accelerated Depreciation:

$1,350,000 x 0.25 = $337,500

This $337,500 will be depreciated over shorter time frames (5, 7, or 15 years), giving you immediate tax deductions in Year 1. Additionally, the remaining building value of $1,012,500 will continue to be depreciated over 27.5 years, providing an annual depreciation deduction of $36,818.

Total Depreciation Deduction in Year 1:

$337,500 (accelerated) + $36,818 (regular depreciation) = $374,318

Now, let's calculate the tax savings for a high-net-worth investor in the 37% tax bracket.

Year 1 Tax Savings:

$374,318 x 0.37 = $138,497

This means that in Year 1 alone, cost segregation allows you to reduce your taxable income by $374,318, resulting in tax savings of $138,497.

Impact on Cash Flow and Wealth Building

By taking these substantial tax savings in Year 1, high-net-worth investors can significantly increase their cash flow. This cash can be reinvested into additional properties, used to pay down existing mortgages faster, or allocated toward other wealth-building ventures.

Cost segregation also boosts the long-term profitability of your real estate portfolio by allowing you to retain more of your rental income, reduce your taxes, and reinvest those savings for exponential growth.

1031 Exchanges: Deferring Capital Gains Taxes to Build Wealth

A 1031 exchange is another powerful tax strategy that allows real estate investors to defer capital gains taxes when they sell one investment property and reinvest the proceeds into another "like-kind" property. For high-net-worth individuals, this strategy is invaluable for scaling their portfolios without the immediate tax burden that typically accompanies property sales.

How a 1031 Exchange Works

When you sell a property, the IRS requires you to pay capital gains taxes on the profit you made from the sale. However, by using a 1031 exchange, you can defer those taxes as long as you reinvest the proceeds into a new property that is of equal or greater value. This strategy allows you to continually upgrade or expand your real estate holdings without losing significant capital to taxes.

Example: Using a 1031 Exchange to Grow Your Portfolio

Let's say you've held one of your new construction properties for 5 years and it has appreciated in value from $300,000 to $375,000. You've built $75,000 in equity during that time, but selling the property outright would trigger capital gains taxes.

Instead of selling and paying taxes, you use a 1031 exchange to defer the taxes and reinvest the $75,000 into a new property worth $450,000. By doing this, you defer the capital gains taxes and leverage your entire $75,000 of equity to acquire a more valuable property—without paying taxes immediately.

This strategy allows you to scale your portfolio faster by keeping your equity working for you, rather than losing a portion of it to taxes. Over time, as you repeat this process with other properties, you can dramatically increase the value of your real estate holdings.

Tax Deferral on a Larger Scale

For high-income investors, the benefits of the 1031 exchange compound as the portfolio grows. Over several decades, by continually deferring taxes through 1031 exchanges, you can build an expansive real estate portfolio worth millions, while legally avoiding capital gains taxes until you ultimately sell the properties—or pass them down to heirs.

The tax deferral provided by 1031 exchanges is one of the most effective ways to keep capital in play while exponentially growing your real estate investments.

Combining Cost Segregation and 1031 Exchanges for Maximum Impact

When combined, cost segregation and 1031 exchanges provide a powerful one-two punch that allows high-net-worth investors to:

1. Minimize Taxes in Year 1: Use cost segregation to front-load depreciation and drastically reduce taxable income, keeping more cash flow in the early years of property ownership.

2. Scale Quickly and Defer Taxes: Use 1031 exchanges to defer capital gains taxes and reinvest the proceeds into larger or higher-performing properties. This keeps your portfolio growing without losing capital to taxes.

Total Wealth Building in Year 1:

Let's revisit the financials from Chapter 5 and add the impact of tax savings from cost segregation and appreciation over time.

- Total Portfolio Value (5 Properties): $1,500,000

- Cash Flow (Net Income from Rent): $24,000/year

- Principal Paydown (Mortgage Amortization): $18,000/year

- Appreciation: $34,500/year (3% appreciation on $1.15M portfolio)

- Tax Savings from Cost Segregation (Year 1): $138,497

Total Wealth-Building Calculation in Year 1:

$24,000 (cash flow)

- $18,000 (principal paydown)

- $34,500 (appreciation)

- $138,497 (tax savings from cost segregation)

<u>Total Wealth Building in Year 1: $215,000+</u>

Long-Term Benefits for High-Net-Worth Investors

By incorporating these tax strategies, high-net-worth investors can maximize cash flow, reduce tax liability, and accelerate the growth of their portfolios. Whether you're building wealth for early retirement, a more comfortable lifestyle, or to pass on to your heirs, using cost segregation and 1031 exchanges together creates a tax-efficient, high-return investment strategy.

Leveraging Tax Strategies for Maximum Wealth Building

For high-net-worth investors, tax planning is just as important as choosing the right properties. By applying cost segregation and 1031 exchanges, you can significantly reduce your tax burden, accelerate your portfolio's growth, and retain more of your income to reinvest.

These strategies provide a powerful framework for long-term wealth building by keeping your money working for you. In the following chapters, we will dive deeper into portfolio scaling, leveraging financing, and protecting your wealth as you continue your journey to financial independence.

This chapter brings together the power of two tax strategies that high-net-worth investors can leverage to exponentially grow their wealth. Feel free to copy and paste this section into your document!

Chapter 7

Financing Strategies for Fast Growth: How to Get Started Even If You Don't Have a Lot of Cash

"Wealth isn't about how much you start with—it's about how wisely you leverage what you have. Strategic financing turns small beginnings into exponential growth."

By now, you understand how powerful the Freedom 5 Formula can be. You've seen how just five properties can create financial freedom and millions of dollars in wealth. But if you're like many readers, you might be wondering: How do I get started if I don't have a huge pile of cash?

This is where creative financing strategies come into play. The good news is, you don't need to have hundreds of thousands of dollars sitting in the bank to begin your journey toward financial freedom. In fact, many successful real estate investors start with very little capital.

In this chapter, we're going to explore the financing strategies that can help you acquire your first few properties, no matter where you're starting financially.

Why Leverage is Your Best Friend

Before we dive into the specific strategies, let's revisit an important concept: leverage. Leverage is the use of borrowed money to increase the potential return on your investment. In real estate, this usually means taking out a mortgage or loan to buy a property, allowing you to control a much larger asset than if you were paying in cash.

Here's why leverage is so powerful: when you finance your properties, you're able to control hundreds of thousands of dollars' worth of real estate for a fraction of the price. For example, with a 25% down payment, you can acquire a $230,000 property for just $57,500 of your own money. The bank finances the rest, but you get to keep 100% of the appreciation, 100% of the cash flow, and all of the tax benefits that come with owning the property.

Leverage allows you to multiply your wealth faster, with less of your own money tied up in the investment.

Traditional Financing: Using Conventional Mortgages

The most common way to finance an investment property is through a conventional mortgage. These loans are similar to the ones you'd use to buy a personal home, but they come with a few key differences when used for investment properties:

• Higher Down Payments: For investment properties, lenders typically require a down payment of 20-25%. This is higher than the 3-5% down payment required for a primary residence, but it also allows you to put skin in the game while letting the bank finance the rest.

• Stricter Lending Criteria: Lenders are often more cautious with investment properties, meaning you'll need to have a good credit score, a stable income, and enough savings to cover the mortgage if the property is vacant for a period.

• Mortgage Interest Rates: Interest rates on investment property loans tend to be slightly higher than those on personal mortgages, but these rates are still historically low, making it a favorable time to lock in financing for your properties.

Leveraging Home Equity: HELOCs and Home Equity Loans

If you already own a home and have built up equity over time, a great way to fund your real estate investments is by tapping into that equity. This can be done through a Home Equity Line of Credit (HELOC) or a home equity loan.

• HELOC: A HELOC is a line of credit secured by your home, allowing you to borrow against your home's equity. Think of it like a credit card with a much lower interest rate. You only borrow what you need, and you can draw from the HELOC as you acquire properties. This is a popular option for real estate investors because it provides flexible financing and can be used for down payments, renovations, or even to buy properties outright.

• Home Equity Loan: Unlike a HELOC, a home equity loan gives you a lump sum of money, which you can then use to invest in real estate. The loan is secured by your home, and you pay it back over time, typically with a fixed interest rate.

Both of these options allow you to leverage the equity you've already built in your home, freeing up cash to invest in income-generating properties.

Seller Financing: Partnering with the Seller to Buy the Property

If you don't have enough cash or can't qualify for traditional financing, seller financing could be a great option. This is a creative strategy where the seller of the property essentially acts as the bank, allowing you to make payments directly to them rather than securing a loan through a traditional lender.

Here's how seller financing works:

• Negotiating Terms: You and the seller agree on the purchase price, the interest rate, and the repayment terms. This could mean making monthly payments to the seller until the property is paid off or until you can refinance with a traditional loan.

• Less Strict Lending Requirements: Sellers are often more flexible than banks when it comes to credit scores or down payments, making this a great option for investors who may not qualify for traditional financing.

• Faster Closing Process: Because you're working directly with the seller, the closing process can be much faster and less complicated than going through a bank.

Seller financing can be especially beneficial in markets where sellers are motivated and willing to negotiate, allowing you to acquire properties even if you're short on capital.

Private Money Lenders: Borrowing from Individuals

Another option for financing your real estate investments is to borrow from private money lenders. These are individuals—rather than banks or financial institutions—who are willing to lend you money to buy properties. Private lenders are often friends, family members, or other investors who want to earn a higher return on their money than they could get from a traditional investment.

Here's why private money lending can be a great option:

• Flexibility: Private lenders can offer much more flexible terms than banks. You can negotiate interest rates, repayment schedules, and down payment requirements directly with the lender.

• Speed: Private money can often be accessed more quickly than bank loans, allowing you to move fast on investment opportunities.

• Creative Terms: You may be able to structure a deal where you pay the private lender a percentage of the profits, rather than interest, which can help reduce your monthly payments and increase your cash flow in the early stages of ownership.

Private money lending is a great option for investors who have a solid deal but may not have enough cash or credit to secure traditional financing.

Hard Money Loans: Short-Term Financing for Investors

If you're looking to acquire a property quickly and plan to refinance or sell it within a short time frame, a hard money loan might be the solution. Hard money loans are typically short-term loans (usually 6-24 months) used by real estate investors to acquire and renovate properties.

Here's why hard money loans are useful:

• Quick Approval: Hard money lenders focus more on the value of the property than your credit score, which means you can get approved and funded much faster than with traditional loans.

• Flexible Terms: Like private lenders, hard money lenders can offer more flexible terms than banks. You can often negotiate repayment schedules and interest rates that fit your investment strategy.

• Great for Fix-and-Flips: Hard money loans are popular among investors who are buying distressed properties, renovating them, and then selling them for a profit. However, they can also be used to fund the purchase of rental properties that you plan to refinance later.

The downside to hard money loans is that they come with higher interest rates and fees than traditional loans. However, if you're in need of fast, short-term financing, they can be a valuable tool in your investment toolbox.

Tapping into Retirement Accounts: Self-Directed IRAs

If you have a retirement account, such as a 401(k) or IRA, you can use it to invest in real estate through a self-directed IRA. This allows you to grow your retirement savings while also building your real estate portfolio.

Here's how it works:

• Self-Directed IRA: Unlike traditional IRAs, which limit your investment options to stocks, bonds, and mutual funds, a self-directed IRA allows you to invest in a wide range of assets, including real estate.

• Tax-Deferred Growth: When you use a self-directed IRA to invest in real estate, all rental income and capital gains are tax-deferred, meaning you don't pay taxes until you withdraw the funds during retirement.

• Diversification: Using your retirement account to invest in real estate gives you another way to diversify your portfolio, reducing your reliance on the stock market.

Investing in real estate through a self-directed IRA can be a great way to build wealth for retirement while taking advantage of the stability and cash flow that real estate offers.

Partnerships: Teaming Up to Share the Investment

If you don't have enough cash or credit to buy a property on your own, consider partnering with someone who does. Partnerships are a common way for new investors to get started in real estate without needing a large amount of upfront capital.

Here's how partnerships can work:

• Pooling Resources: You and your partner pool your money and credit to buy the property together. You might split the down payment, mortgage payments, and cash flow, or one partner might provide the capital while the other manages the property.

• Sharing Responsibilities: One partner might focus on finding and managing the property, while the other provides the financing. This can be a great way to get into real estate if you have the time and knowledge but not the cash.

• Win-Win: Partnerships allow both parties to benefit from the deal. The partner who brings the financing can earn passive income without having to manage the property, while the partner handling the day-to-day operations gains experience and equity in the investment. This kind of arrangement is a great way to leverage each other's strengths and get into the game, even if one partner has less capital to invest.

Example of a Partnership in Action:

Let's say you find a great new construction rental property, but you don't have the full 25% down payment required for the mortgage. Instead of missing out on the opportunity, you approach a friend or colleague who's interested in real estate but doesn't want the responsibility of property management. You agree to split the profits 50/50, with your partner providing the down payment and you managing the property.

You handle the tenant screening, maintenance, and day-to-day operations, while your partner provides the capital. Both of you benefit from the property's cash flow and long-term appreciation, and you've successfully acquired a property that would have been out of reach otherwise.

Don't Let a Lack of Cash Hold You Back.

The biggest takeaway from this chapter is simple: don't let a lack of cash hold you back from building wealth through real estate. There are so many financing options available, from traditional mortgages to creative strategies like seller financing and private money loans. Even if you don't have a lot of money to start, there are ways to get into the game.

Remember, the key to building wealth through the Freedom 5 Formula is leveraging other people's money (whether it's the bank's, a partner's, or a private lender's) to acquire income-generating properties. You don't need to have millions to build a million-dollar portfolio—all you need is the right strategy and a willingness to think outside the box.

Next Steps: Start Building Your Team

In the next chapter, we're going to dive into the importance of building a strong real estate team. Whether it's real estate agents, property managers, contractors, or financial advisors, the people you surround yourself with can make or break your success in real estate investing.

By the end of the next chapter, you'll know exactly who you need on your team and how to find the best people to help you execute the Freedom 5 Formula.

Chapter 8

Building Your Dream Team: The Key to Real Estate Success

"Success doesn't happen in isolation. Surround yourself with experts who elevate your vision and turn it into reality."

If you want to succeed in real estate and truly maximize the potential of the Freedom 5 Formula, you need to surround yourself with the right people. Real estate is a team sport, and having a group of trusted professionals working alongside you is essential to achieving long-term financial freedom.

No matter how experienced or knowledgeable you are, trying to handle everything on your own will only slow you down and increase the likelihood of making costly mistakes. The good news is, you don't have to do it alone. With the right team in place, you can focus on growing your portfolio and reaching financial independence, while your team handles the day-to-day tasks and keeps things running smoothly.

In this chapter, we're going to cover the key players you need on your real estate dream team, how to find them, and how to work together to execute the Freedom 5 Formula.

The Essential Members of Your Real Estate Team

Here's a breakdown of the essential team members who will help you achieve your real estate goals. Each one plays a specific role in ensuring that your investments are profitable and well-managed. Let's meet your dream team.

1. Real Estate Agent (Your Property Finder)

The first person you'll need on your team is a real estate agent who specializes in investment properties. This agent will be your go-to source for finding and evaluating potential properties in your target market.

Here's why having the right real estate agent is critical:

• Market Expertise: A good real estate agent knows the local market inside and out. They can guide you toward high-growth areas, help you identify properties with the best potential for appreciation, and steer you away from bad deals.

• Access to Listings: Real estate agents often have access to properties before they hit the market. This gives you a competitive edge when it comes to finding deals in high-demand areas.

• Negotiation Skills: A skilled real estate agent will negotiate on your behalf to get the best possible price and terms for your investment properties. This can make a big difference in your ability to create positive cash flow from day one.

When choosing a real estate agent, look for someone with experience working with investors. Ask them how many investment properties they've helped clients acquire and if they own any rental properties themselves. You want someone who understands your goals and can help you make smart investment decisions.

2. Property Manager (Your Day-to-Day Operator)

Once you've acquired your properties, you'll need a property manager to handle the day-to-day operations. Unless you plan to manage the properties yourself (which is a full-time job), hiring a good property manager is essential to maintaining your cash flow and ensuring your properties run smoothly.

Here's what a property manager will do for you:

• Tenant Screening: A good property manager will find and screen tenants, ensuring you get reliable renters who pay on time and take care of the property.

• Rent Collection: They'll handle rent collection and ensure that you get paid on time every month.

• Maintenance and Repairs: Property managers coordinate maintenance, repairs, and any necessary improvements to keep your properties in good condition.

• Vacancy Management: If a tenant moves out, your property manager will work quickly to fill the vacancy, minimizing the time your property sits empty.

A strong property manager is a critical part of your real estate team. They free you from the burden of managing the property yourself, allowing you to focus on growing your portfolio. When choosing a property manager, look for someone with a proven track record of managing rental properties in your area.

Ask for references and take the time to read reviews from other landlords.

3. Mortgage Broker or Lender (Your Financing Expert)

Next up is your mortgage broker or lender. This person plays a vital role in securing the financing you need to acquire your properties. Whether you're using conventional mortgages, private lenders, or other creative financing options, your mortgage broker or lender will guide you through the process and help you find the best terms for your loans.

Here's what your mortgage broker or lender will do:

• Help You Secure Financing: They'll find the right loan products for your situation, whether it's a conventional mortgage, an FHA loan, or a more creative financing option.

• Guide You Through the Process: From pre-approval to closing, your mortgage broker will handle all the paperwork and ensure that everything runs smoothly.

• Negotiate Better Rates and Terms: A good mortgage broker has relationships with multiple lenders and can shop around to get you the best possible rates and terms for your investment properties.

When choosing a mortgage broker, look for someone who has experience working with investors and understands the unique needs of financing rental properties.

They should be familiar with investment property loans and be able to guide you on the best strategies for leveraging your financing.

4. Real Estate Attorney (Your Legal Expert)

A real estate attorney ensures that all of your transactions are legally sound and that your interests are protected. While not every transaction requires an attorney, having one on your team will give you peace of mind, especially when dealing with complex transactions like seller financing or partnerships.

Here's how a real estate attorney can help you:

• Reviewing Contracts: They'll review purchase agreements, lease contracts, and any other legal documents to ensure that everything is in your best interest.

• Handling Closings: In some states, real estate attorneys handle the closing process and ensure that all documents are properly executed.

• Solving Legal Issues: If any legal issues arise with tenants, title disputes, or zoning laws, your attorney will help you navigate these challenges and protect your investment.

Choose an attorney who specializes in real estate and has experience working with investors.

They should understand the nuances of property transactions, tenant law, and real estate tax strategies.

5. Contractor (Your Property Improvement Pro)

At some point, you'll likely need to make improvements or repairs to your properties. That's where a trusted contractor comes in. Whether you're doing a simple repair, a renovation, or a full rehab, having a reliable contractor on your team is crucial to maintaining and increasing the value of your properties.

Here's what a contractor can do for you:

• Repairs and Maintenance: A contractor can handle regular maintenance tasks like fixing leaks, repairing appliances, or replacing worn-out fixtures.

• Renovations: If you're investing in properties that need updates, a contractor can help you renovate to increase the property's value and rental potential.

• Emergency Repairs: When things go wrong, you want a contractor who can respond quickly and get the issue resolved with minimal disruption to your tenants.

When choosing a contractor, look for someone who is licensed, insured, and experienced in working with investment properties.

Ask for references and get multiple quotes for larger projects to ensure you're getting a fair price.

6. Accountant (Your Tax Strategist)

A real estate accountant is essential to help you navigate the financial side of your investments, particularly when it comes to taxes. Real estate offers significant tax advantages, but you need an accountant who knows how to maximize those benefits while keeping you compliant with the law.

Here's how an accountant will support your success:

• Tax Deductions: Your accountant will ensure that you're taking full advantage of the tax benefits of real estate, such as depreciation, mortgage interest deductions, and operating expense write-offs.

• Record Keeping: They'll help you track your income and expenses to ensure you're accurately reporting your earnings and paying the correct amount of taxes.

• Tax Planning: A good accountant will help you plan for the future, ensuring that you're structuring your investments in a way that minimizes taxes and maximizes your cash flow.

When choosing an accountant, look for someone with experience working with real estate investors.

They should be well-versed in the tax code as it relates to rental properties and be able to offer advice on structuring your investments for maximum tax efficiency.

How to Find the Best People for Your Team

Now that you know who you need on your real estate team, the next step is finding the right people. Here are a few tips to help you build a team of professionals who will support your success:

• Network with Other Investors: One of the best ways to find quality professionals is to ask other real estate investors for recommendations. Networking at local real estate meetups, conferences, or online forums can help you connect with experienced agents, property managers, contractors, and more.

• Do Your Homework: Don't just go with the first person you meet. Take the time to research each professional, read reviews, check references, and interview them to make sure they're a good fit for your needs.

• Build Long-Term Relationships: Once you find a great team member, work on building a long-term relationship with them. The more you work together, the better they'll understand your goals and how to help you achieve them.

You're Not Alone in This Journey

Remember, real estate is a team effort. You don't have to do everything yourself.

By surrounding yourself with the right professionals, you'll be able to scale your portfolio faster, avoid costly mistakes, and focus on what really matters—achieving financial freedom through the Freedom 5 Formula.

Chapter 9

Property Management and Maintenance—The Key to Consistent Cash Flow

"Take care of your property today, and it will take care of you for years to come. Consistent management today ensures lasting wealth tomorrow."

You've built your team, secured financing, and acquired your first properties. Now what?

Owning investment properties is only the beginning. To ensure consistent cash flow and long-term profitability, you need to focus on property management and maintenance.

How you manage your properties and care for them will ultimately determine your success as a real estate investor. This is where many investors either thrive or fail, and getting it right is essential for achieving the financial freedom you're aiming for with the Freedom 5 Formula.

In this chapter, we're going to cover the best practices for managing your properties, keeping tenants happy, and ensuring that your investments continue to generate strong returns year after year.

Why Good Property Management is Critical

Let's start with a simple truth: your property is only as good as the tenants living in it. No matter how great your location or how perfect the market, if your property isn't well-managed, you'll end up dealing with late payments, vacancies, and costly repairs. A well-run property, on the other hand, leads to steady cash flow, satisfied tenants who stay for the long term, and minimal stress.

Here's why good property management matters:

• Cash Flow Stability: Proper management ensures that rents are collected on time and that your property remains fully occupied. This stability is key to creating the steady, reliable cash flow that powers the Freedom 5 Formula.

• Tenant Retention: Happy tenants are more likely to renew their leases, saving you the hassle and cost of finding new tenants. A well-managed property leads to satisfied renters, which means fewer vacancies and reduced turnover.

• Lower Maintenance Costs: Staying on top of routine maintenance prevents small issues from turning into costly repairs. Proactive property management can save you thousands of dollars in the long run.

Whether you decide to manage your properties yourself or hire a property management company, the goal is the same: to keep your tenants happy, your properties in good condition, and your cash flow consistent.

Self-Management vs. Hiring a Property Manager

One of the first decisions you'll need to make is whether you want to manage your properties yourself or hire a professional property manager. Both options have their pros and cons, and the right choice will depend on your goals, time availability, and comfort level with handling tenants.

Self-Management

If you decide to manage your properties on your own, you'll be responsible for everything—from screening tenants and collecting rent to handling maintenance requests and solving tenant issues. This can be a rewarding experience if you enjoy being hands-on, but it can also be time-consuming and stressful, especially if you own multiple properties.

Pros of Self-Management:

• Cost Savings: You'll save money by not having to pay a property management fee (which is typically 8-10% of your rental income).

• Direct Control: You have complete control over how your property is managed, how tenants are selected, and how issues are handled.

• Hands-On Learning: Managing your own properties gives you valuable experience and insight into the day-to-day operations of being a landlord.

Cons of Self-Management:

• Time-Consuming: Managing properties can be a full-time job, especially if you have multiple rentals or difficult tenants.

• Handling Tenant Issues: You'll be responsible for handling tenant complaints, late payments, and any disputes that arise.

• Maintenance and Repairs: You'll need to coordinate maintenance and repairs yourself, which can be stressful if you don't have a reliable contractor on call.

Hiring a Property Manager

If you prefer a more hands-off approach, hiring a professional property manager is a great option. A property manager will handle all of the day-to-day tasks for you, from finding tenants to collecting rent and coordinating maintenance. This allows you to focus on growing your portfolio and enjoying the passive income your properties generate.

Pros of Hiring a Property Manager:

• Less Stress: The property manager handles all tenant issues, rent collection, and maintenance requests, freeing you from the headaches of day-to-day management.

• Expertise: A professional property manager has experience handling all aspects of rental property management and can likely do it more efficiently than you could on your own.

• More Time: By delegating property management, you free up your time to focus on acquiring more properties, enjoying your passive income, or pursuing other passions.

Cons of Hiring a Property Manager:

• Cost: Property managers typically charge a percentage of your rental income (8-10% is standard), which can eat into your cash flow.

• Less Control: You'll have less direct control over how your property is managed and how tenant issues are handled.

• Quality Varies: Not all property managers are created equal, and a bad property manager can lead to more headaches than managing the property yourself. That's why it's crucial to choose wisely.

Keeping Tenants Happy—The Key to Long-Term Success

One of the most important aspects of successful property management is keeping your tenants happy. Happy tenants pay their rent on time, take care of the property, and are more likely to stay for the long term, which reduces vacancy rates and increases your cash flow.

Here are some tips for maintaining good relationships with your tenants and keeping them satisfied:

• Communicate Clearly: From the beginning, set clear expectations with your tenants. Make sure they understand the lease terms, how to submit maintenance requests, and what's expected of them as tenants.

• Respond Quickly: One of the top reasons tenants become dissatisfied is when landlords or property managers are slow to respond to maintenance requests or complaints. Make it a priority to address issues quickly and professionally.

• Provide a Quality Living Environment: Regularly inspect your properties and ensure that they are well-maintained and safe. Small upgrades like fresh paint or new appliances can go a long way in making tenants feel valued and comfortable in their home.

• Respect Their Privacy: Always respect your tenants' privacy and give proper notice before entering the property for repairs or inspections.

• Reward Good Tenants: If you have long-term tenants who consistently pay their rent on time and take care of the property, consider offering incentives like small rent discounts or upgrades to encourage them to stay longer.

Handling Maintenance and Repairs

Proper maintenance is crucial for keeping your properties in good condition and avoiding costly repairs down the line. Whether you're managing the property yourself or working with a property manager, it's important to have a system in place for handling maintenance issues quickly and efficiently.

Here are some best practices for keeping up with property maintenance:

• Create a Maintenance Schedule: Regularly inspect key components of the property, such as HVAC systems, plumbing, and roofing, to ensure that everything is in good working order. Preventative maintenance can save you thousands of dollars in the long run.

• Build a Reliable Network of Contractors: If you're self-managing, make sure you have a list of reliable contractors you can call for repairs. This includes plumbers, electricians, handymen, and landscapers. Having a strong network will make it easier to handle maintenance issues as they arise.

• Set Aside Funds for Repairs: Unexpected repairs are a part of owning rental properties, so it's important to budget for them. A good rule of thumb is to set aside 1-2% of the property's value each year for maintenance and repairs.

• Stay on Top of Tenant Requests: If a tenant submits a maintenance request, don't let it sit. Even small issues like a leaky faucet can turn into bigger problems if left unresolved. Promptly addressing maintenance requests shows tenants that you care about the property and their comfort.

Minimizing Vacancies

Vacancies are one of the biggest threats to your cash flow. Every month your property sits empty is a month you're losing money. Fortunately, there are several strategies you can use to minimize vacancies and keep your properties fully occupied:

• Market Your Property Effectively: Use high-quality photos and detailed descriptions to market your rental property online. List it on popular rental platforms and consider offering virtual tours to attract more prospective tenants.

• Screen Tenants Carefully: One of the best ways to avoid vacancies is to screen tenants carefully upfront. Look for tenants with stable income, good rental histories, and positive references. A reliable tenant is more likely to stay for the long term.

• Offer Competitive Rent: Make sure your rent is in line with the local market. Charging too much can drive away potential tenants, while charging too little can hurt your cash flow. Research the local market to find the sweet spot.

• Consider Lease Renewals: Proactively reach out to tenants a few months before their lease ends to discuss renewal. Offering small incentives, like a slight rent discount or a minor upgrade, can encourage tenants to renew their lease rather than move out.

Long-Term Property Management Success

Managing your properties effectively is key to maximizing cash flow and building long-term wealth. Whether you choose to manage the properties yourself or hire a property manager, your goal should be to create a smooth, efficient system that keeps your tenants happy, your properties well-maintained, and your income flowing steadily.

By focusing on tenant satisfaction, routine maintenance, and minimizing vacancies, you can ensure that your properties remain profitable for years to come. This is how you sustain the success of the Freedom 5 Formula and keep your real estate empire growing.

Next Steps: Growing Your Portfolio

In the next chapter, we'll dive into the strategies for scaling your portfolio once you've successfully managed your first few properties.

Chapter 10

Scaling Up: How to Grow Your Real Estate Portfolio for Maximum Wealth

"Scaling your real estate portfolio is about more than just acquiring properties—it's about strategically building a foundation for limitless wealth. Growth happens when every move is made with purpose."

"Wealth built over time is the kind that lasts. Be patient with the process, for every day your wealth compounds, and your future grows brighter."

By now, you've laid the foundation for your financial freedom with the Freedom 5 Formula—you've acquired your first five new construction investment properties, established consistent cash flow, and built equity. The next step in your journey is scaling your portfolio to grow your wealth even further. This chapter will focus on how to expand strategically without the hassle of rehabbing properties, as the Freedom 5 Formula is built around the benefits of new construction investments.

Scaling doesn't mean taking on massive risk—it means using the solid foundation you've built and reinvesting wisely to grow your portfolio while maintaining stability.

Here's how you can grow your real estate empire with minimal risk while sticking to new construction properties.

Why Scaling Your Portfolio Is the Key to Building Wealth

Before diving into the "how," let's revisit why scaling up is so important in real estate:

• Increased Cash Flow: Each additional property you acquire adds to your monthly cash flow. With multiple properties generating rental income, you create a reliable stream of passive income that fuels further investments.

• Equity Growth: New construction properties offer strong appreciation potential in growing markets. As your properties appreciate in value over time and your tenants pay down your mortgages, your equity increases.

• Diversification: As you grow your portfolio, you're spreading your risk. If one property has a vacancy or unexpected issue, the others can continue to generate income, which helps stabilize your overall cash flow.

Scaling your portfolio is about multiplying the success of your first five properties, using proven strategies that focus on long-term growth without the added risk of rehabilitating distressed properties.

The 3 Pillars of Scaling with New Construction Properties: Leverage, Equity, and Cash Flow

Let's focus on the three pillars that will allow you to scale effectively using new construction properties—leverage, equity, and cash flow.

1. Leverage: Using Financing Wisely to Scale Faster

One of the most powerful advantages of real estate is the ability to use leverage—borrowing money to acquire properties. With new construction properties, financing is more favorable than for older or distressed properties, as lenders see them as lower risk. You can use leverage to scale your portfolio in several ways:

• Cash-Out Refinancing: As your new construction properties appreciate and your tenants pay down the mortgage, you build equity. A great strategy to scale is to refinance your properties once you've accumulated enough equity. A cash-out refinance allows you to access that equity and use it as the down payment for additional properties. This way, you're using the bank's money to grow your portfolio while keeping your initial capital intact.

• Leveraging Your Cash Flow: As you accumulate positive cash flow from your properties, you can reinvest it into new construction deals. Each time you acquire a new property, your rental income increases, which gives you more capital to reinvest in future deals. Over time, this snowballs into greater cash flow and a larger portfolio.

• Favorable Loan Terms for New Construction: Lenders tend to offer better financing terms for new construction properties because they are lower risk, require less maintenance, and tend to appreciate more predictably. By sticking with new construction, you not only minimize upfront costs but also secure more attractive interest rates and loan terms, which help you scale more efficiently.

2. Equity: Building Wealth Through Appreciation and Principal Paydown

Equity growth is a key factor in scaling your portfolio. New construction properties, especially in high-growth markets, tend to appreciate steadily, which means your equity builds quickly. Additionally, each month your tenants are paying down your mortgage, which further increases your equity.

Here's how you can use your equity to scale:

• Refinance to Unlock Equity: After holding your properties for a few years, you'll likely have built significant equity. By refinancing, you can pull out a portion of this equity to invest in additional properties without having to sell your original assets. This way, you can continue to benefit from appreciation on the first property while using the equity to fund new investments.

• Accelerate Mortgage Paydown with Extra Cash Flow: One of the advantages of new construction properties is that they typically have lower maintenance costs, which can result in higher cash flow. You can use that extra cash flow to pay down your mortgages faster, building equity even more quickly. Once your mortgage is paid off, your cash flow increases dramatically, giving you even more resources to scale your portfolio.

By focusing on equity growth and strategically refinancing, you can continue to expand your real estate holdings without needing significant new capital.

3. Cash Flow: Fueling Your Growth with Rental Income

The beauty of new construction properties is that they tend to attract high-quality tenants and offer steady cash flow from the outset. Once you've established your initial portfolio, you can use the cash flow from those properties to fuel your growth.

Here are some ways to use your cash flow strategically:

• Reinvest for Future Properties: One of the simplest ways to grow your portfolio is to reinvest your cash flow into new properties. As your rental income increases, you can save for the down payment on your next new construction investment. Each new property you acquire adds more cash flow to your bottom line, which accelerates your ability to invest further.

• Pay Off Mortgages Faster: By using a portion of your cash flow to accelerate mortgage paydown, you reduce your debt load and increase your equity. Once your properties are paid off, your cash flow skyrockets, which allows you to either live off the passive income or reinvest it in additional properties.

• Increase Rental Income Over Time: With new construction properties, you can raise rents over time as the market grows, further boosting your cash flow. By staying in markets with high growth potential, you'll ensure that your rental income continues to rise, which fuels future expansion.

Scaling Without the Hassle of Rehabs

Unlike the BRRRR strategy, which relies on buying distressed properties, rehabilitating them, and refinancing, the Freedom 5 Formula focuses on new construction for a reason—less hassle. Here's why sticking to new construction as you scale makes sense:

• Low Maintenance Costs: New construction properties come with fewer maintenance issues, as everything is brand new and often covered by warranties. This means fewer unexpected repairs and lower maintenance costs, which allows you to keep more of your cash flow.

• Attractive to Long-Term Tenants: Tenants prefer new construction properties because they offer modern amenities, energy efficiency, and overall better living conditions. As a result, you're more likely to attract long-term tenants who will take care of the property and stay longer, reducing turnover costs.

• No Rehab Headaches: By focusing on new construction, you avoid the time, effort, and risk involved in rehabbing distressed properties. Instead, you can scale efficiently by simply acquiring well-located, high-quality properties and letting time and tenant payments work in your favor.

Scaling Strategies That Work for New Construction Investors

Now that you know how to leverage your equity, financing, and cash flow, let's look at some practical strategies for scaling your portfolio with new construction properties:

1. Slow and Steady Growth

If you prefer a conservative approach, focus on reinvesting your cash flow and refinancing existing properties every few years. This allows you to acquire one or two new properties at a time, building your portfolio steadily while minimizing debt and risk.

2. Leverage Strategic Refinancing

As your properties appreciate and you build equity, you can strategically refinance them to pull out equity and use that for new down payments. This allows you to scale faster without needing additional capital from your savings. By maintaining reasonable loan-to-value ratios, you can grow your portfolio without overleveraging.

3. Reinvest for Compounding Growth

Once you've established strong cash flow, use that income to pay down your mortgages faster or reinvest it into new properties. The goal is to keep reinvesting your profits to maximize compounding returns—each new property generates more cash flow, which in turn allows you to acquire even more properties.

Scaling for Long-Term Success

The key to scaling with the Freedom 5 Formula is to stick with new construction properties and use strategic financing and equity-building tactics to grow your portfolio.

By focusing on cash flow, equity growth, and leverage, you can continue to build wealth without the added risks and challenges of rehabilitating older properties.

As you scale your portfolio and grow your wealth through new construction properties, it's essential to understand why focusing on single-family homes and duplexes is the best path forward.

These property types offer unmatched stability, consistent cash flow, and appreciation potential compared to more complex real estate investments like multifamily units or REITs.

In the next chapter, we'll dive into why sticking with residential real estate—specifically single-family homes and duplexes—ensures reliable, long-term success.

Chapter 11

Why Single-Family Homes and Duplexes Outperform Multifamily and REITs

"Homes are more than structures—they are the building blocks of financial stability. Residential real estate gives you control, consistency, and wealth for life."

As real estate investors, we're often bombarded with different strategies, property types, and investment vehicles to choose from.

While multifamily properties and Real Estate Investment Trusts (REITs) have their advantages, one of the most reliable paths to consistent returns and long-term success remains residential real estate, particularly single-family homes (SFHs) and duplexes.

In this chapter, we'll dive deep into why single-family homes and duplexes consistently outperform multifamily properties and REITs when it comes to generating reliable cash flow, long-term appreciation, and ease of management.

We'll explore how sticking to this core strategy can provide you with the consistent, dependable results needed to make the Freedom 5 Formula work.

The Predictability and Stability of Single-Family Homes and Duplexes

When it comes to real estate investing, stability and predictability are crucial factors. While larger multifamily properties and REITs may seem appealing for their scale, single-family homes and duplexes offer a level of stability and predictability that multifamily properties often cannot.

Here's why:

1. Strong Demand from a Broad Tenant Base

- Single-family homes and duplexes are always in demand because they cater to a broad range of tenants—families, young professionals, retirees, and everyone in between.

- People will always need a place to live, and single-family homes are generally more appealing to long-term tenants. Duplexes, too, offer more space and privacy compared to multifamily apartments, making them attractive to tenants who are seeking stability.

- This constant demand translates into lower vacancy rates and more consistent rental income. Multifamily properties, while lucrative during periods of high demand, tend to experience higher turnover and vacancies, especially in times of economic uncertainty or overbuilding in the market.

2. Less Exposure to Market Volatility

- Single-family homes and duplexes are more insulated from market volatility than multifamily properties. In a downturn, multifamily units may experience higher vacancies or rent reductions as tenants move to more affordable housing or double up with family or roommates. Single-family homes, however, tend to retain tenants who are seeking stability and are less likely to move frequently.

- Moreover, single-family homes are often located in suburban neighborhoods, which tend to be less volatile compared to urban markets, where large multifamily properties are concentrated.

Suburbs also tend to attract more stable, long-term tenants such as families and working professionals.

3. Easier to Sell and Liquidate

- When the time comes to sell, single-family homes and duplexes offer more flexibility and a larger pool of potential buyers. You're not just selling to investors, but also to owner-occupants, which widens the market for resale and ensures that you can liquidate your assets more easily if necessary.

- Multifamily properties, on the other hand, are typically sold to other investors, limiting your potential buyer pool and making it harder to sell in certain market conditions.

- Single-family homes, in particular, benefit from strong appreciation driven by demand from both owner-occupants and investors. This dual market dynamic makes SFHs a powerful long-term investment vehicle.

The Performance of Single-Family Homes vs. Multifamily Properties

Let's look at how single-family homes (and duplexes) consistently outperform multifamily properties in key areas:

1. Higher Appreciation Rates

- Historically, single-family homes appreciate faster than multifamily properties. This is due in part to the fact that single-family homes are influenced by owner-occupant demand, which drives prices higher, especially in desirable neighborhoods.

- Multifamily properties, by contrast, are primarily valued based on their income potential (cap rates), which can stagnate during times of high vacancies or rent pressure. They rely heavily on local rental demand, whereas single-family homes benefit from overall housing demand, which can be stronger and more diversified.

- This appreciation is especially valuable when using strategies like the Freedom 5 Formula, where long-term growth in property value can exponentially increase your wealth over time.

2. Lower Turnover and Vacancy Rates

- One of the most significant advantages of single-family homes and duplexes is the lower tenant turnover compared to multifamily properties. Families and professionals who rent single-family homes or duplexes tend to stay longer, often for years, especially if they have children enrolled in local schools or jobs nearby.

- Multifamily units, on the other hand, tend to attract more transient tenants—students, young professionals, and people who may not be as financially stable. This results in higher turnover rates, which leads to higher vacancy periods and more frequent maintenance costs from preparing units for new tenants.

- The stability of tenants in single-family homes and duplexes leads to more reliable cash flow and fewer expenses related to vacancy and turnover.

3. Easier and Cheaper to Finance

- Financing for single-family homes and duplexes is generally easier to obtain and comes with better terms compared to multifamily properties. This is because traditional lenders view single-family homes as a lower risk asset class due to their strong demand and resale potential.

- Interest rates on loans for single-family homes are typically lower than those for multifamily properties, which improves your overall cash flow and makes it easier to manage your debt load.

- Duplexes, while slightly more complex than single-family homes, still qualify for favorable financing terms, especially for first-time investors using traditional or FHA loans.

The Advantages of Single-Family Homes Over REITs

While Real Estate Investment Trusts (REITs) offer a way to invest in real estate without directly owning properties, they come with their own set of limitations when compared to owning physical assets like single-family homes and duplexes.

1. Limited Control

- When you invest in REITs, you're putting your money into a pooled investment controlled by fund managers. You have no say over which properties are bought, sold, or how they're managed.

- With direct ownership of single-family homes and duplexes, you maintain full control over your investments—you decide where and what to buy, how to manage your properties, and when to sell.

2. Lack of Tax Benefits

- One of the biggest advantages of direct real estate ownership is the tax benefits. With single-family homes and duplexes, you can take advantage of deductions for mortgage interest, depreciation, repairs, and even certain travel expenses related to property management.

These deductions significantly reduce your taxable income and boost your returns.

- REITs, by contrast, don't offer the same tax advantages. While they do pay dividends, which can provide income, those dividends are often taxed at a higher rate than the passive income generated from rental properties.

3. Lower Long-Term Appreciation

- REITs are heavily influenced by stock market fluctuations and often don't appreciate at the same rate as directly owned real estate. They provide steady dividends but lack the long-term appreciation potential that single-family homes or duplexes offer, especially in growth markets.

- With single-family homes, you benefit from both rental income and property appreciation, giving you a dual source of wealth accumulation.

Why Sticking to the Freedom 5 Formula Works

The Freedom 5 Formula focuses on single-family homes and duplexes because these property types consistently offer the best combination of cash flow, appreciation, and ease of management. By sticking to this strategy, you can build a portfolio that is stable, easy to manage, and provides long-term wealth-building opportunities.

Here's why sticking to the Freedom 5 strategy with single-family homes and duplexes works so well:

1. Predictable Cash Flow

- Single-family homes and duplexes offer consistent cash flow from reliable, long-term tenants. This predictability is key to building financial freedom, as it provides a steady income you can rely on month after month.

2. Easier to Manage

- Managing a portfolio of single-family homes and duplexes is generally simpler and less labor-intensive than managing large multifamily properties. With fewer tenants to deal with, fewer maintenance issues, and lower turnover, single-family homes are ideal for investors who want passive income without the stress of complex property management.

3. Proven Long-Term Success

- The combination of strong appreciation, consistent demand, and favorable financing terms make single-family homes and duplexes the perfect vehicles for long-term success. By focusing on these properties, you're building a stable, resilient portfolio that will grow over time, both in terms of cash flow and equity.

The Reliable Path to Wealth

While multifamily properties and REITs have their place in certain investment strategies, single-family homes and duplexes offer the ideal balance of stability, ease of management, and strong returns. By sticking to the Freedom 5 Formula and focusing on residential real estate, you're positioning yourself for consistent success.

In the next chapter, we'll explore how to sustain this momentum and continue growing your portfolio for long-term financial freedom.

Chapter 12

Sustaining Momentum and Managing Growth

"Long-term success isn't about how fast you grow, but how well you manage that growth. Stay focused, stay disciplined, and let your wealth build itself."

As your real estate portfolio expands, you'll face new challenges—managing multiple properties, staying organized, and maintaining cash flow at scale. The goal of this chapter is to help you sustain momentum without becoming overwhelmed, and to provide tips on streamlining your operations so your real estate empire continues to run smoothly.

When you first started out, managing one or two properties might have been relatively easy. But as you add more properties to your portfolio, the complexity increases. Managing five, 10, or 15 properties requires a systematic approach, smart delegation, and efficient processes.

Building Systems to Scale Your Portfolio

The key to managing a growing real estate portfolio is building systems that allow you to scale efficiently. Whether you're handling property management, maintenance, or finances, putting the right systems in place will help you stay organized and ensure that everything runs smoothly.

Here are a few areas where you should focus on building scalable systems:

1. Property Management Automation

As your portfolio grows, manual tasks like rent collection, maintenance requests, and tenant communications can quickly become overwhelming. Automating these processes can save you time and reduce the risk of human error. Here's how:

• Rent Collection: Use online platforms that allow tenants to pay rent electronically. This reduces the likelihood of late payments and makes rent collection seamless.

• Maintenance Requests: Set up an online portal where tenants can submit maintenance requests. This makes it easier to track requests and ensures that nothing falls through the cracks.

• Lease Management: Use property management software to track lease renewals, rent increases, and tenant agreements. This will help you stay organized and prevent issues from arising due to expired leases or missed rent hikes.

2. Delegating to Your Team

As your portfolio grows, the need for a trusted team becomes even more important. By delegating tasks to your team—whether it's property management, contractors, or accountants—you free up your time to focus on higher-level investment decisions.

• Outsource Property Management: If you're still self-managing your properties, consider hiring a property manager as your portfolio expands. The time saved can be better spent on finding new deals or improving existing properties.

• Delegate Maintenance: Develop relationships with reliable contractors who can handle repairs and maintenance without your direct involvement. This ensures that issues are addressed quickly while keeping you from getting bogged down with day-to-day tasks.

3. Financial Tracking and Planning

Staying on top of your finances is crucial as you scale your portfolio. Without proper financial tracking, it's easy to lose track of expenses, miss tax deductions, or overlook opportunities for refinancing or reinvestment.

• Use Accounting Software: Invest in software that allows you to track your income, expenses, and cash flow in real time. This will give you a clear picture of how each property is performing and help you make informed decisions.

• Plan for Growth: As you scale, develop a plan for reinvesting profits, paying down mortgages, and expanding your portfolio. Having a long-term financial strategy ensures that your growth is sustainable and aligned with your goals.

Avoiding Common Pitfalls as You Scale

With growth comes new challenges. While scaling your portfolio offers exciting opportunities, it also comes with potential pitfalls. Here are a few common mistakes to watch out for as you grow:

1. Over-Leveraging

As tempting as it may be to acquire properties quickly, over-leveraging —taking on too much debt—can put your entire portfolio at risk. Make sure that each property generates enough cash flow to cover its mortgage, maintenance, and other expenses. Avoid relying too heavily on appreciation or future refinancing to make deals work.

2. Neglecting Maintenance

As you add more properties, it's easy to let maintenance slip through the cracks. However, neglecting regular upkeep can lead to costly repairs down the line and hurt your cash flow. Create a maintenance schedule and stick to it, or delegate this responsibility to your property manager.

3. Failing to Reinvest

Once your portfolio starts generating significant cash flow, it's important to continue reinvesting that income into new properties or paying down existing mortgages. Failing to reinvest can slow your growth and limit your ability to reach financial independence.

Maintaining Momentum with the Freedom 5 Formula

At this point, you've built a solid foundation, scaled your portfolio, and created systems to manage your growth. The next step is to maintain your momentum and continue building wealth over time. The Freedom 5 Formula is designed to be sustainable for the long term, and by staying disciplined with your investments, you'll continue to see your wealth grow.

Remember: real estate is a long-term game. The rewards compound over time, and by staying focused on your goals, reinvesting profits, and managing your properties efficiently, you're on the path to financial freedom.

Next Steps: Unlocking Your Full Potential in Real Estate

As we approach the final chapters, we'll explore why real estate investing is within reach for anyone willing to take action—and why some people never take the leap. Success in real estate isn't reserved for a select few; it's available to those who commit, get educated, and take strategic steps forward.

We'll also dive into how working with experts like SDIRA Wealth can streamline your journey, helping you avoid costly mistakes and accelerate your path to financial freedom. By leveraging the experience and resources of a dedicated team, you can focus on building your wealth while they handle the complexities.

If you're serious about achieving financial independence through real estate, the next two chapters will show you exactly why the right mindset and the right partnerships can make all the difference.

Chapter 13

Why Everyone Can Invest in Real Estate (But Some People Won't)

"Excuses keep you stuck, but action moves you forward. The key to success in real estate—and in life—is letting go of the reasons why you can't and embracing the belief that you can."

Real estate is one of the most accessible, proven, and stable pathways to wealth. Time and time again, it has been shown that anyone—no matter their background, financial situation, or experience—can build significant wealth by investing in real estate. And yet, despite its numerous advantages, many people never take the leap.

What holds them back? Often, it's not a lack of resources or opportunity but a set of limiting beliefs, excuses, and mindsets that prevent them from moving forward.

Let's explore the most common excuses people make and the flawed thinking that holds them back from building financial freedom through real estate investing.

1. Excuse: "I Don't Have Enough Money to Start"

One of the most pervasive excuses is the belief that you need a lot of money to invest in real estate. Many people think they need tens of thousands of dollars in savings to even consider buying a property. While having cash reserves is certainly helpful, this mindset overlooks the power of leverage.

The truth is, you don't need to have the full purchase price of a property saved up. In fact, most successful investors use other people's money—through mortgages, partnerships, or creative financing—to acquire real estate. You can start with as little as 5-10% down, or even less with specific loan programs, and leverage the bank's money to build your wealth. The barrier to entry is much lower than many believe.

2. Excuse: "The Market Is Too Unpredictable"

The fear of market volatility often holds people back from investing in real estate. They worry about property values dropping, economic downturns, or other unpredictable factors that could impact their investment. While these concerns are understandable, they're also part of every investment.

The key to overcoming this mindset is to understand that real estate is a long-term game. Property values might fluctuate in the short term, but over the long term, real estate has historically appreciated in value. Unlike the stock market, which can experience wild day-to-day swings, real estate tends to be much more stable. If you choose the right markets and invest for the long haul, you can ride out short-term dips and come out ahead in the long run.

3. Excuse: "I Don't Have Time"

Many people shy away from real estate investing because they believe it will require too much time and effort. They picture themselves dealing with tenants, handling repairs, or constantly managing their properties.

This is where building a strong team becomes crucial. With a good property manager and real estate team in place, you can make real estate investing hands-off. Property managers handle the day-to-day operations, from finding tenants to managing repairs, allowing you to focus on your career or other priorities while your investments generate passive income. Real estate can be as time-consuming—or as passive—as you want it to be.

4. Excuse: "It's Too Risky"

Real estate is often perceived as risky by those who haven't done their homework. They might have heard horror stories about bad tenants, expensive repairs, or market crashes and concluded that investing in real estate isn't worth the risk.

While every investment carries some degree of risk, real estate offers multiple layers of protection. First, properties are tangible assets that don't disappear if the market crashes. Second, you can mitigate risk by choosing high-demand markets, performing due diligence on properties, and setting aside reserves for unexpected expenses. Real estate investing is risky only when you go in unprepared. With the right knowledge and a strategic approach, you can minimize risk and maximize returns.

5. Excuse: "I Don't Know Enough"

Another common mindset that holds people back is the fear of not knowing enough about real estate investing. Many people feel overwhelmed by the perceived complexity of buying, managing, and financing properties, so they never take the first step.

The solution is simple: educate yourself. There are countless resources—books, courses, podcasts, and mentors—that can help you learn the basics of real estate investing. You don't need to know everything before you start, but you do need to be willing to learn as you go. Many successful investors started with little to no experience and built their knowledge through action. Don't let the fear of not knowing enough stop you from getting started.

6. Excuse: "I'm Waiting for the Perfect Time"

The idea that there's a "perfect time" to invest is another major roadblock. Some people wait for the right market conditions, lower interest rates, or a better financial situation before they start investing. The problem is, there's rarely a perfect time for anything, and waiting often leads to missed opportunities.

The best time to start investing in real estate is when you're ready to commit to the process. Property values and interest rates will always fluctuate, but the power of real estate comes from time in the market, not timing the market. The longer you wait, the longer you delay your wealth-building journey.

7. Excuse: "I'm Afraid of Failure"

Fear of failure is one of the most powerful reasons people hesitate to invest. They worry about making a mistake, losing money, or facing unexpected challenges. But failure is often part of the journey—and it's through these failures that investors learn and grow.

Successful investors embrace failure as a learning opportunity. They understand that mistakes are part of the process, and they don't let fear hold them back from taking action. If you're willing to learn from your mistakes and keep moving forward, failure becomes a stepping stone to success, not a roadblock.

The Mindset Shift: From Excuses to Action

At the heart of every excuse is a mindset that keeps people stuck in their current situation. The belief that real estate is too risky, too complicated, or out of reach holds countless individuals back from achieving financial freedom. But the truth is, anyone can invest in real estate if they're willing to shift their mindset from fear and excuses to action and learning.

The Freedom 5 Formula is built on the idea that real estate investing is accessible to anyone, regardless of their financial background or experience. Whether you're starting with a small amount of capital or looking to grow a large portfolio, this formula is designed to guide you through the process step by step.

What separates those who succeed in real estate from those who don't is not access to resources or opportunities—it's the mindset. The people who take action, even when they don't feel fully prepared, are the ones who ultimately achieve financial freedom.

Final Thoughts

Real estate investing isn't reserved for the wealthy or the lucky—it's for anyone who's willing to take control of their financial future. The biggest hurdle is often our own mindset. Once you let go of the excuses, the opportunities for wealth-building through real estate are endless.

The question is, are you ready to stop making excuses and start building the life you deserve?

Every day you wait is another day you delay your financial freedom.

The time to start is now.

Chapter 14

Accelerating Your Success with SDIRA Wealth: Why Partnering with Experts Makes All the Difference

"Success is amplified when you're guided by experts. With the right team, you don't just invest—you thrive, grow, and achieve financial independence faster than you ever thought possible."

By now, you have a solid grasp of how the Freedom 5 Formula can guide you toward financial freedom. You've learned how to build, scale, and manage a real estate portfolio efficiently. But what if you could accelerate the process, avoid common pitfalls, and maximize your results by partnering with a team of experts who specialize in real estate investing? Imagine creating time freedom today as you build wealth—without taking on another full-time job to manage the intricacies of real estate investing.

Here's the good news: you don't have to do it all yourself. By leveraging the power of a full-service team that has everything in place, you can continue enjoying your current career, spend quality time with your family, and build your portfolio with less effort.

With a team like SDIRA Wealth, you gain access to exclusive new construction properties optimized for the Freedom 5 Formula, strategically located in the best growth markets in the country. SDIRA

Wealth boasts a proven track record of success, spanning over 20 years, with the expertise, experience, and systems in place to ensure your real estate journey is seamless.

From creating a customized investment plan to executing it with step-by-step guidance, SDIRA Wealth's team will take care of the heavy lifting for you.

They handle everything, including finding the right properties, arranging financing, and preferred management teams in place that work with your rentals. With SDIRA Wealth by your side, you can focus on what truly matters—living the life you want today while building a future of financial independence.

In this final chapter, we'll show you how working with SDIRA Wealth can take your real estate journey to the next level. By partnering with professionals who have decades of experience and a proven strategy, you can streamline your path to financial freedom and unlock the full potential of the Freedom 5 Formula—all without sacrificing your time or peace of mind.

The Power of Partnering with Experts

Building a successful real estate portfolio on your own is possible, but why do it the hard way? Partnering with experts can drastically shorten your learning curve, help you avoid costly mistakes, and give you the confidence to make smarter, faster investment decisions. That's where SDIRA Wealth comes in. They offer a unique, full-service real estate team that handles every aspect of investing—from property selection to financing and ongoing management.

Imagine being able to access exclusive opportunities, grow your wealth, and achieve financial freedom—all while letting a team of seasoned professionals guide you every step of the way.

Why Partnering with SDIRA Wealth Gives You the Best Advantages from Day 1:

1. Access to Exclusive Properties

One of the most significant advantages of working with SDIRA Wealth is their access to exclusive build-to-rent properties that are not available on the open market. These properties are located in high-growth markets, strategically selected and designed to deliver positive cash flow from day one.

You won't have to compete with the general public or sift through endless listings. SDIRA Wealth's exclusive access means you get first pick on high-performing properties, ensuring your portfolio is positioned for success from the start. This gives you a competitive edge over other investors and sets you up to grow your portfolio faster with the right properties.

One of the standout advantages of partnering with SDIRA Wealth is the ability to leverage their volume of new construction builds. With over 20 years of experience and a significant track record in the market, as developers SDIRA Wealth has cultivated relationships with manufacturers,, suppliers, and contractors that provide access to exclusive pricing and bulk discounts—benefits that individual investors would struggle to achieve on their own.

By partnering with a team that builds in scale, you automatically gain access to bulk buying power. This means you're not only getting a handpicked property in a high-growth market, but you're also acquiring it at the best possible price.

SDIRA Wealth's negotiation leverage allows them to secure better deals on construction costs, materials, and financing rates, which translates into instant value for you as an investor.

2. Streamlined Investment Process

SDIRA Wealth is beyond turnkey company by offering solutions and customized programs for investors. They handle every part of the process—from assisting with property selection that match your needs and financing to inspections and closing. You won't need to worry about navigating the complex maze of financing negotiations, trying to win a bidding war, , or trying to find reputable contractors.

They've streamlined the entire process, so you can focus on big-picture strategy and scaling your investments, while they take care of the details. The hassle of finding, vetting, and purchasing properties is taken off your shoulders, giving you the freedom to concentrate on your career and personal life while still building wealth.

3. Professional Property Management

Managing rental properties can be time-consuming and stressful—especially when you're juggling a full-time career or other commitments. Finding tenants, handling repairs, and managing leases can quickly become overwhelming.

SDIRA Wealth has professional property management teams in place in each market that you can choose from, ensuring your properties are well-maintained without the headaches of being a landlord. You'll have peace of mind knowing that your investments are in expert hands, and you can truly enjoy the passive income your properties generate.

4. Tax Optimization Strategies

One of the most overlooked benefits of real estate investing is the significant tax advantages it offers. SDIRA Wealth's team includes tax experts who specialize in helping you maximize the tax benefits of your investments. Whether it's depreciation, cost segregation, or utilizing 1031 exchanges, they will guide you through strategies that reduce your tax burden and increase your net returns.

This means you'll keep more of your profits in your pocket to reinvest and grow your portfolio, accelerating your path to financial freedom. By minimizing your taxes, SDIRA Wealth ensures that your investment dollars work harder for you.

5. Long-Term Wealth-Building Support

Unlike some services that focus only on the transaction, SDIRA Wealth is committed to your long-term success. Their support doesn't end after you acquire your properties—they provide ongoing education, regular updates on market conditions, and personalized investment strategies to help you continue building wealth over the years.

They know that the journey to financial freedom is not just about acquiring properties; it's about sustaining growth, adapting to market changes, and continuously improving your portfolio. With over 23 years of experience, they've helped countless investors succeed, and they'll be there for you as you navigate your own path to financial independence.

Save Time, Avoid Mistakes, and Maximize Your Returns

By partnering with SDIRA Wealth, you're not just getting access to excellent properties—you're gaining a dedicated team of real estate professionals who are invested in your success. They take the guesswork out of real estate investing, allowing you to save time, avoid costly mistakes, and maximize your returns.

With SDIRA Wealth, you're able to bypass the steep learning curve that often comes with real estate investing. Instead, you'll benefit from their years of expertise, insider knowledge of the best markets, and their proven strategies to build wealth faster. They've helped countless investors achieve financial freedom, and they're ready to help you do the same.

Your Path to Financial Freedom Starts Here

If you're serious about taking the next step toward financial independence, SDIRA Wealth is here to guide you. Whether you're just getting started with real estate or looking to scale an existing portfolio, their team of experts will create a customized plan tailored to your goals. By working with a full-service team that handles everything from property selection to management, you can enjoy the freedom and benefits of real estate investing—without the overwhelming time commitment.

SDIRA Wealth provides a clear advantage for investors by offering access to exclusive properties, a streamlined investment process, professional management, and tax-optimization strategies, all backed by decades of experience. It not only saves you time but also helps you avoid mistakes and maximize returns—making it a perfect solution for investors ready to take the next step toward financial freedom.

Now is the time to take action. Whether you're a seasoned investor or just starting your journey, SDIRA Wealth offers the tools, experience, and access to exclusive opportunities that will put you on the fast track to financial freedom.

Don't wait.

Book a call with their team today and see how easy it can be to start building your future wealth.

Final Thoughts

The Power of the Freedom 5 Formula

The Freedom 5 Formula is more than just a strategy—it's a proven pathway to achieving the financial freedom and stability that so many seek but rarely find through traditional investing.

By focusing on new construction properties, building just five strategically selected investments, and leveraging the immense benefits of cash flow, appreciation, principal paydown, and tax advantages, you are setting yourself up for a future of security and success.

We've walked you through the key pillars of the Freedom 5 Formula— how to select the right properties, the importance of leveraging expert support like SDIRA Wealth, and how advanced tax strategies such as cost segregation and 1031 exchanges can accelerate your wealth building. Throughout this journey, you've seen how it's possible to build significant equity, generate passive income, and secure long-term wealth with a simple, repeatable approach.

But what makes the Freedom 5 Formula truly special is that it's designed to work for anyone—whether you're a seasoned investor or just starting out. It's about making smart, strategic moves that allow you to unlock the potential of real estate without sacrificing your time or making costly mistakes. By prioritizing long-term wealth building, you're laying the foundation for sustainable financial growth.

Over time, as your investments appreciate, consistent cash flow becomes a natural byproduct—allowing your income to grow steadily while you enjoy the freedom and lifestyle you've created.

The next step is yours. You now have the knowledge and tools to transform your financial future through real estate. With the Freedom 5 Formula, the path to financial independence is not just possible—it's within your reach. Whether you decide to take this journey on your own or partner with experts like SDIRA Wealth, the most important thing is to take action.

 Your financial freedom starts now, and with the right plan, it will last a lifetime.

You've got the Freedom 5 Formula—now it's time to put it into action! Whether you're just getting started or looking to scale your investments, we're here to help you build lasting wealth through smart real estate strategies.

Let's Talk! Schedule a free consultation with our team and discover how SDIRA Wealth can help you maximize your investment potential.

Visit us at <u>SDIRAwealth.com</u> to book your complimentary Financial Freedom Call!